GW00506743

The Good and the Beautiful

MY FIRST
AFRICA READER

Written by Jenny Phillips
and Maggie Felsch

Cover illustration by Farah Shah

Map of Africa illustrated by Kessler Garrity and
Nada Serafimovic

goodandbeautiful.com

TABLE OF CONTENTS

BOOK 1

OX

CVC Words

The Good and the Beautiful

This story takes place in Niger.

NIGER

An ox got hot.

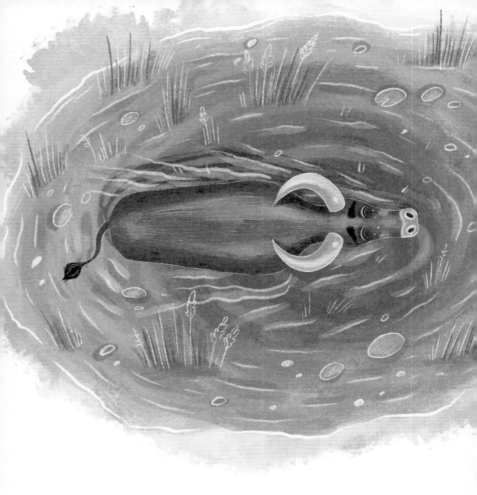

It can get wet.

Mud, mud, mud!

An ox can fit.

It got mud on a mat.

Bad ox!

Hut

CVC Words

The Good and the Beautiful

This story takes place in Nigeria.

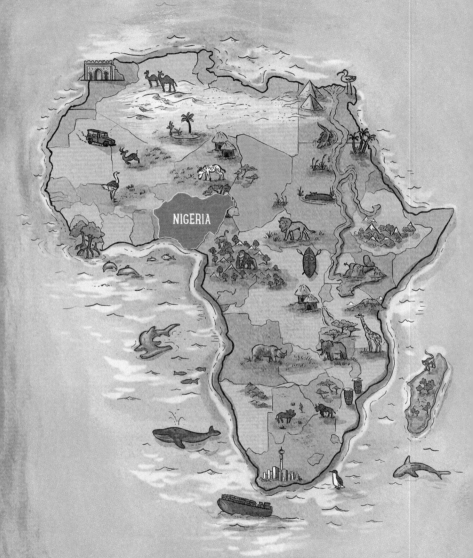

NIGERIA

I am at a hut.

I can hug it!

Can I fix it?

Yes! I can get on top.

A cat did not get wet.

It can sit on a red mat.

Pot

BOOK 3

CVC Words

The Good and the Beautiful

This story takes place in Malawi.

MALAWI

Mom got a big pot.

Let it get hot.

Mom can dip it.

I got a lot!

We Love Mom

Sight Words: Group 1

The Good and the Beautiful

This story takes place in South Africa.

Story illustrated by Bojana Stojanovic

He can mix the jam.

She can cut the yam.

I go to bed.

She can hug me.

We love Mom a lot.

Ben Has a Hen

Words Where S Says /Z/

The
Good AND THE Beautiful

This story takes place in Zambia.

ZAMBIA

Ben has a pet.

It is a hen.

It is not as big as a dog.

It was on a log.

Ben got it.

It is in the pen.

BOOK 6

The Sun Is Up

CVC Words

The Good and the Beautiful

This story takes place in Namibia.

Story illustrated by Yana Zybina

goodandbeautiful.com

The sun is up.

The sun is not up.

I am in bed.

41

The sun is up.

It is hot.

The sun can set.

Dad and I sit.

We go in.

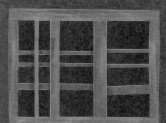

The sun is not up.

The sun is up. I get up.

Is It Hot?

CVC Words

This story takes place in Tanzania.

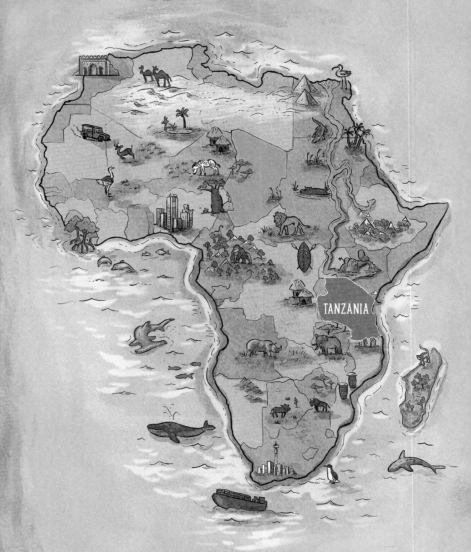

We love to dig.

We dig a pit.

I set a big log in it.

Is it hot? Not yet.

Mom can get it hot.

Dad can set the big
pot on top!

A Jog

Sight Words: Group 2

The Good and the Beautiful

This story takes place in the
Democratic Republic of the Congo.

DEMOCRATIC
REPUBLIC
OF THE CONGO

We are on a jog.

We go up, up, up!

It is so hot.

We look for Dot.

She had to get a sip.

Look! She is so wet.

This story takes place in Kenya.

Story illustrated by Yana Zybina

© 2022 The Good and the Beautiful, LLC

goodandbeautiful.com

Look at the hog.

Is it a mom or a dad?

Look! She is the mom.

The dad hog is so big.

He has a nap.

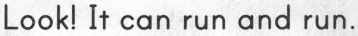

Look! It can run and run.

The Tall Wall

CK; ALL

The Good and the Beautiful

This story takes place in Cameroon.

I pick up the ball.

I kick it by the wall.

I look for it.

It is on the tall wall!

Can I get it back?

She can get it!
She has a tall neck.

Dik-Dik

Ending Consonant Blends

The Good and the Beautiful

This story takes place in Somalia.

SOMALIA

She is a dik-dik.

She can run as fast
as the wind.

She is not big at all,

but she must get a sip.

At last she can rest in the soft sand.

The Ball

SS, FF, LL

The
Good AND THE Beautiful

This story takes place in Angola.

ANGOLA

I toss the ball to him.

I miss! It falls in the pond.

"I will get it!" he yells.

He got it!

He will pass it to me.

It is a wet mess!

BOOK 13

The Cliff

Beginning Consonant Blends;
Short Words with Y

The Good AND THE Beautiful

This story takes place in South Africa.

SOUTH AFRICA

Story illustrated by Jennifer Falkner

My mom and I get to the cliff.

Will we try to go up it?

No!

We stop and rest in the dry grass.

We look at a black duck.

It can fly by in the sky!

My Day

AY

The
Good AND THE Beautiful

This story takes place in Uganda.

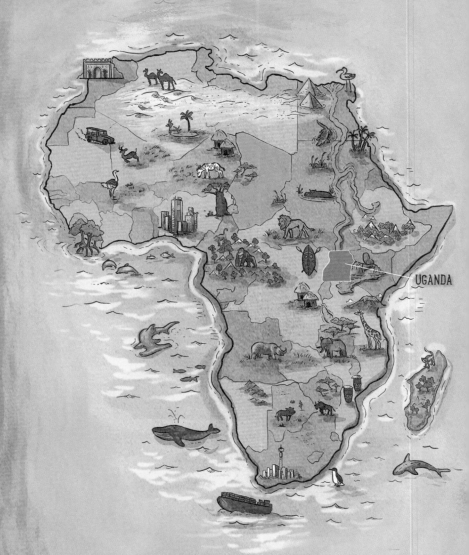

UGANDA

Story illustrated by Zoe Damoulakis

© 2022 The Good and the Beautiful, LLC

goodandbeautiful.com

I get up and pray.

I get hay for the pigs.

I help stack the clay bricks.

I stay at my desk.

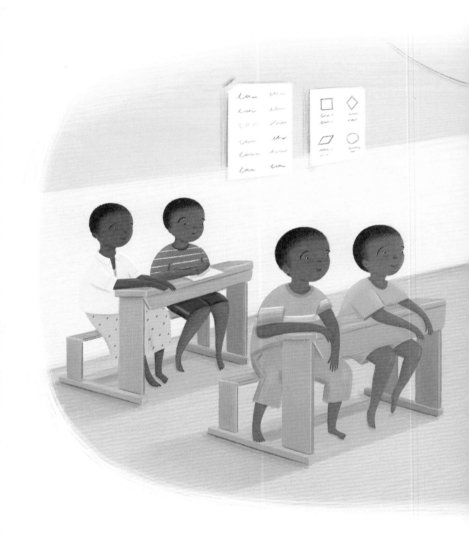

I try my best.

Yay! I can play!

They Pray

Sight Words: Group 3

This story takes place in Ghana.

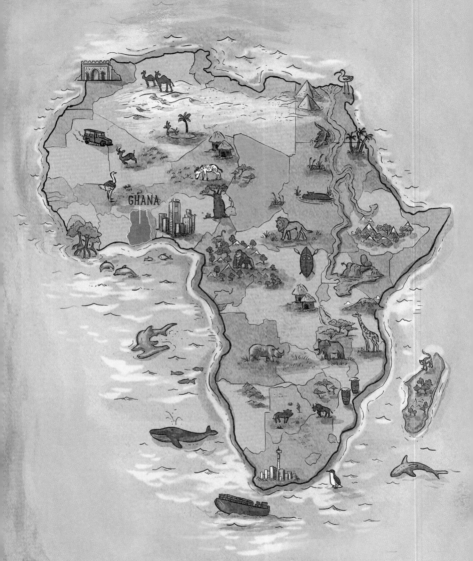

Story illustrated by Raquel Martin

© 2022 The Good and the Beautiful, LLC

goodandbeautiful.com

A boy and girl pray at the end of the day.

A dad and two little boys sit.

They pray.

117

Oh no, a little girl is lost!

Does she pray?

Yes, and God helps.

BOOK 16

The Big Ship

SH

The Good and the Beautiful

This story takes place in Namibia.

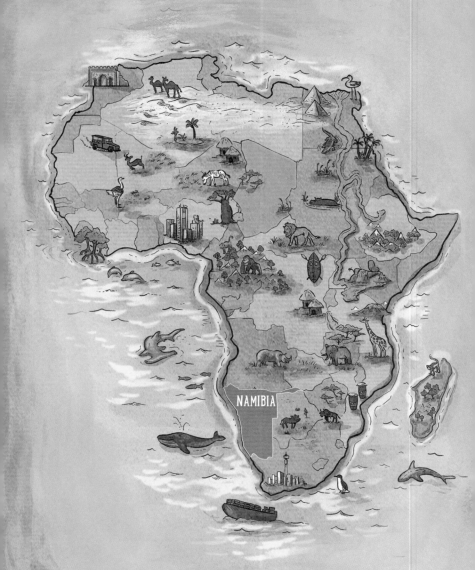

NAMIBIA

Story illustrated by Tania Rex

© 2022 The Good and the Beautiful, LLC

goodandbeautiful.com

My dad is on the ship.

The net has a lot of fish.

Dad looks at a crab.

It has a red shell.

Flash! The ship will go back.

Chad

CH

This story takes place in Chad.

CHAD

This is a map of Chad.

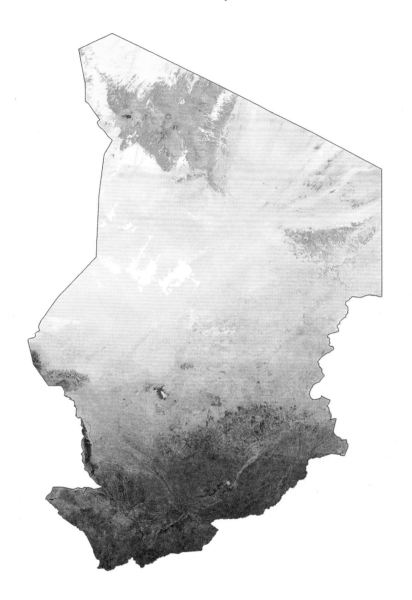

It can be hot and dry in Chad.

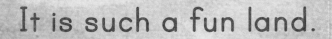

It is such a fun land.

There is so much to see.

The boy has lunch.

His mom will chop the fish.

They love Chad so much.

BOOK 18

Tut

TH

The Good and the Beautiful

This story takes place in Morocco.

This is Tut.

He is on the path.

Mom goes with him.

Tut does math.

He loves it!

Then he plays.

It Is Singing

ING

The Good AND THE Beautiful

This story takes place in Botswana.

BOTSWANA

It is singing.

They are flying.

It is resting.

Look! That fox is jumping.

Look! It is running fast!

sheep

EE

This story takes place in Tunisia.

I feed the sheep.

They need grass and hay.

This sheep has a weed.

We keep them in a big pen.

Seeds

Sight Words: Group 4

This story takes place in Sierra Leone.

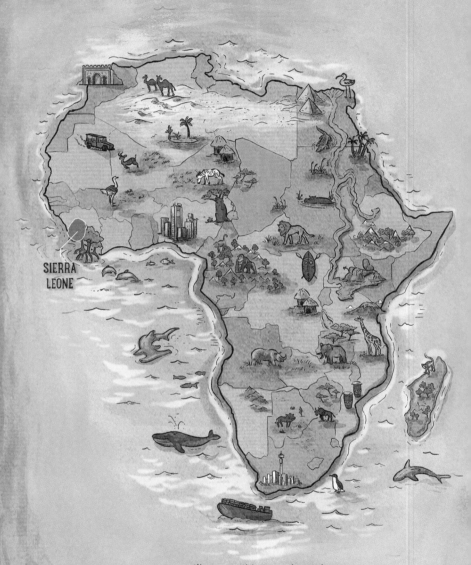

SIERRA LEONE

Story illustrated by Sandra Eide

goodandbeautiful.com

"Can plants come from little seeds?" I ask.

"Put some seeds in the pot," Dad tells me.

Many days come and go.

I do not see any plants yet.

"Look what is in your pot,"
Dad tells me one day.

We Helped

ED

This story takes place in Liberia.

LIBERIA

Tom was sick, so we helped him.

I planted seeds.

Sam picked up trash.

Dad fixed things.

Mom filled the jug
at the well.

Try these nature readers from The Good and the Beautiful!

My First Nature Reader
By Jenny Phillips

My Second Nature Reader
By Jenny Phillips

My Third Nature Reader
By Jenny Phillips and
Maggie Felsch

goodandbeautiful.com